MY TOWN

Sidewalk detail, Albuquerque

MY TOWN

A Memoir of
Albuquerque, New Mexico
in Poems, Prose and Photographs

by

MARGARET RANDALL

With a Foreword by John Nichols

WingsPress

San Antonio, Texas
2010

My Town: a memoir of Albuquerque, New Mexico in poems, prose and photographs © 2010 by Margaret Randall

Cover image: *Interior of Church, Pecos* (Photograph by Margaret Randall)

First Edition

Print Edition ISBN: 978-0-916727-73-4
ePub ISBN: 978-1-60940-003-3
Kindle ISBN: 978-1-60940-004-0
PDF ISBN: 978-1-60940-005-7

Wings Press
627 E. Guenther
San Antonio, Texas 78210
Phone/fax: (210) 271-7805

On-line catalogue and ordering:
www.wingspress.com
All Wings Press titles are distributed to the trade by
Independent Publishers Group
www.ipgbook.com

Library of Congress Cataloging-in-Publication Data:

Randall, Margaret, 1936-
  My town : a memoir of Albuquerque, New Mexico in poems, prose
and photographs / by Margaret Randall ; with a foreword by John
Nichols. -- 1st ed.
      p. cm.
  "All Wings Press titles are distributed to the trade by Independent
Publishers Group."
   ISBN 978-0-916727-73-4 (pbk. : alk. paper) -- ISBN 978-1-
60940-003-3 (epub) -- ISBN 978-1-60940-004-0 (kindle) -- ISBN
978-1-60940-005-7 (library pdf)
  1. Albuquerque (N.M.)--Literary collections. I. Title.
  PS3535.A56277M9 2010
  811'.54--dc22
                                    2010004348

For my brother, John

Contents

Sidewalk detail, Albuquerque *   *frontispiece*

Foreword, by John Nichols   *ix*

Time Found Me: An Introduction   *xiii*

De Anza Motor Lodge   2
A Sadness of Plywood   3
Real Children Staring Back   5
La Placita, Old Town   7
Nothing Was What It Pretended   8
Community Center, Buena Vista & Coal   10
Friday Night at the Community Center   11
Dad's Metronome   13
Old Bordelon   16
Perfect Is Always What I Saw   17
Paris Was Where We Wanted to Dance   19
Downtown Albuquerque, Kimo Theater   21
Before Sputnik   22
I Was Alone That Night   24
Albuquerque High School, 1947   26
Decreasing the Property Values   27
The Sorting Hat   28
This Could Have Happened   30
Until There Were No More Bottle Caps   31
Volcano and Mesa   34
Two Deaths   35
Road to Volcano Cones   36
Gay Meant Have a Good Time   37
Before Pink   39
Have Some Dessert   41
Above the Colors of a Dirndl Skirt   43
Petroglyph National Park   46

* Photograph titles are in italics. Unless otherwise noted,
  all photographs are by Margaret Randall.

Swaying Left	47
Kiva, Coronado State Monument	48
Favorite Places	49
Jefferson Junior High, 1947	50
Send Coyote Down	51
Weapon of Mass Destruction 1	53
Weapon of Mass Destruction 2	55
Lovelace Hospital, 1953	56
Who Knows What Experiments	57
Where We Were	61
Theater of the Absurd	62
Startling these Skies in 1054	64
Alvarado Hotel, 1930	66
Sad Replica	67
Transportation Center, Albuquerque	68
The Houses Look the Same	69
Flames Draw the Heat	71
An Attitude I Never Learned	72
Among the Arugula and Spinach Dip	74
Intersection of Central and Second Street	75
Petroglyph National Park	76
Sam	77
Penitente Morada	84
Weapon and Signature	85
Elaine	87
Elaine de Kooning, 1980s	89
Downtown Albuquerque, art nouveau detail	94
Women I Would Never Be	95
Eva's Corn	96
Unburdened	97
Tent Rocks, north of Albuqerque	98
Verdant	99
La Luz	100
The Shorter Script	102
Ever Ready to Fly	103
Dream Me	105
The Thumb, Sandia Mountains	106
About the Author	107

Foreword

They say you can't go home again, but that's not always true. Margaret Randall left her Albuquerque childhood and traveled truly far away, experiencing many extraordinary adventures of the body, soul, and conscience while maturing in a way that few of us are bold enough to imagine, let alone attempt. Margaret's "outside" world was one of artistic and political activism and complex personal relationships that took place in New York, Europe, Mexico, Cuba, Nicaragua. Then, at age 48, she came back to Albuquerque and has been here ever since.

Nostalgia is a tricky emotion: Upon reflection, the past is rarely what it seemed to be at the time. If we are blest—and conscious—as we grow older, we learn to see things not only for what they are but for what they used to be. With luck we may come to understand our personal histories along with the true nature of our universal roots.

Margaret Randall's life history is one of curiosity that has impelled constant discovery . . . and rediscovery. This passionate book discovers and rediscovers Albuquerque when it was a "quiet" town after the Second World War until just before Vietnam. During that era Margaret was lively, timid, a prankster, confused, and eager to grow. Bound to tradition and uncertain of how to escape, she peered under rocks and questioned authority, wondering about New Mexico's atomic secrets and its racial and gender issues. In these poems, photographs, and prose portraits of friends and family, she describes not only what she loved in Albuquerque but also what was hiding underneath.

Margaret the impetuous adolescent climbed over motel walls to skinny dip in swimming pools, and she set tires afire atop a volcano west of town in hopes of causing an urban panic à la Orson Welles. Both shy and aggressive, she challenged some things and let other stuff slide. Wanting to be "normal," she kept veering toward "different." She yearned to escape the small-town atmosphere but did not know how. Finally, she got married and fled to Spain, yet returned when the money ran out . . . and then the marriage did too. So finally Margaret was gone again, off to the races for real.

When she returned to Albuquerque in 1984 she was scorned and rejected by the U.S. government and then re-assimilated after a bitter legal battle. It required five years, a slew of lawyers, and many financial donations for Margaret to reclaim her roots, her family, her New Mexico—past and future. She is a woman who truly fought for her right to be home.

Margaret claims to be the only non-musical (i.e. tone deaf!) person in her family, yet as a child she loved her father's metronome, little realizing that she too had a remarkable musicality that lay in the rhythm of her words which have tumbled out, now, for decades, singing songs in many different registers heard round the world.

Years ago, on the empty mesa outside Albuquerque, Margaret learned that alone does not mean to be lonely. Decades later, after her return, that knowledge blossomed into her love affair with landscape touched briefly by a peregrine falcon, or by the distant bark of a coyote, or by the persistent silhouette of Sandia Peak that suddenly, approaching old age, she managed to actually climb.

The book is a loving gift to family and the place where they lived . . . and continue living still beyond parents who have died. It's an elegy to place, history, and culture, to innocence (and ignorance) that have evolved to a macroscopic understanding of how the world works. There are poems to petroglyphs and sopaipillas, Juárez bullfights, atomic bombs and conquistadors, old-time movie theaters and a fear of being gay. Toward the end she describes her ascent of La Luz Trail on Sandia Peak, a journey that took a lifetime and whose memory is "planted in every poem."

There's also a moment when UNM visiting professor, the artist Elaine de Kooning, looks Margaret straight in the eye and ushers her " . . . into a larger world, a dimension I've inhabited since. It was a world in which the most generous ideas were nurtured and what was off-limits for many seemed matter of fact." (p. 91)

That's what this book is about.

—John Nichols
Author of *The Milagro Beanfield War*

Time Found Me:
An Introduction

(O)ne day, driving through routine streets, everything shifted. Change unmasked itself along tree-lined residential blocks, houses I hadn't stepped inside for decades, nondescript or impertinent façades, whole neighborhoods erased by development. Images of Albuquerque when I was a child—1940s, '50s and '60s—pushed to the surface, landsweeping human and natural configurations and allowing me to see back through vertical layers rather than horizontally.

These poems were born on a double-take. Of a piece I understood how this desert city shaped my childhood and adolescence, embraced the young white Scarsdale transplant at first fearful of difference then knowing her life depends upon it. Cardinal directions reclaimed me, marked by the scent of sage and piñon forests to the north, baked flatlands to the south, mountains glowing deep pink each afternoon to the east, and the silhouette of dark volcanic cones to the west.

Fifties conformity, secrets we were never meant to know, Cold War bullying, the male entitlement girls and woman endured silently back then, all the confusion and conformity inherent in growing up, escape into first sad marriage, and the birth of a bomb designed to elevate power to ultimate control. But also the land, artists and art, Friday night string quartets, an emerging memory of peoples to whom I am linked by a connective tissue thicker than blood. Those who died young. Those who refuse to die.

Streets and Plazas named for sixteenth century war criminals. Pre-Chicano Hispanics and diverse Indian tribes. African Americans—still calling themselves Negroes—who came with the Railroad and stayed. Pockets of Southeast Asians,

Africans and Indians from India would claim their places many years later. All these inhabitants or their ghosts walk through these poems, as do the individuals who were my parents' friends and mine.

Language shapes how we think and act. But land, cultural memory and social interaction shape language. My own particular white female middle-class transplant, dream-laced, rebellious, color-coded dialog with my origins—staggering between the questions of then and knowledge of now—have brought this book to fruition.

I am grateful for the engaged attention my brother John Randall and my friend Paul Lauter paid these poems; their suggestions made them stronger. Working once again with Bryce Milligan at Wings Press has been exciting; he is a wonderful book designer as well as editor. My life companion Barbara Byers, inhabits this place with me. It is our home. As always, her careful reading and many contributions were invaluable.

MY TOWN

De Anza Motor Lodge, 2009.

A Sadness of Plywood

We didn't know De Anza as a surname of Conquest,
just another set of unfamiliar syllables
in this new place:
"de anza to a tourist's prayer"
my mother joked.

The motel shone on the city's main street, Route 66
once rode the country going west,
Central Avenue as it passed through Albuquerque
its Pachucos and Indians
stoking my adolescent fear.

Our Anglo family of five enjoyed a few nights
of De Anza luxury
before moving to shabbier rooms with kitchenette
Fourth Street's bar-studded thirst
then on to the safety of our uptown home.

For years De Anza stood: beckoning invitation,
signpost
in our arrival script,
bridge to our family's break
with east coast propriety.

Older, I remember dark nights, midnight pranks
with friends
who climbed its pumice wall
slipped naked and gleeful
into its private swimming pool.

We had to stop when one guy's outraged wife
discovered I'd shown my naked body
to her man,
spewed venom across our fifties threshold
demanded I stay away.

Shame held me mute before her screams
and other neighbors' faces
floating in other doorways,
condemnation that would fester
in me for years.

Today De Anza is boarded up,
its smog-stained windows
hidden behind a sadness of plywood.
Today the dead motel is one more ruin
along a strip of empty structures

where summer nights tough women
approach a crawl of low riders,
crack costs a few dirty bills
and the homeless lady walks, brown blanket
pulled about her shoulders.

Once the best promise of a western city,
the old motel's demise
careens near where I turn
to enter today's map,
home that finally feels like home.

In 1947 New Mexico's largest city was a town:
92,000 between the locals
and those arriving with TB and asthma
to its promise of desert cure.

Sixty miles north, Santa Fe wasn't yet home to Hollywood.
City fathers decreed all buildings
mirror native pueblos
while herding real Indians beneath the Plaza's colonnade.

Santa Fe: narrow-laned capitol, piñon-dotted hills.
Albuquerque: railroad stop, post World War II
working-class sprawl. The first elite, pristine,
the second already spreading across the Rio Grande
sucking the aquifer dry.

My parents chose the larger city where Dad sold men's clothing
then earned a diploma to teach.
He bought back the 'cello dispatched in eastern angst,
broke from his Prussian father's strict demands
began a life in music.

Mother thought the waitress at La Placita exotic
and asked her to sit for a portrait in clay.
On weekends we drove to nearby Indian pueblos
traded old clothes for turquoise
collected cacti that filled Dad's fingers
with festering spines.

Those fingers vibrated 'cello strings, held my hand,
could be counted on to comfort, applaud, deliver.

Years later, one freezing January night
they braided mine
as we stood against the first invasion of Iraq.

We grew into this city oblivious to its spliced cultures,
slowly emerged from our white ghetto
to touch and taste, stumble and learn
and one day begin to know.

We visited Acoma's Sky City unaware the name Oñate
proudly worn by schools and parks
belonged to a 16th century war criminal
who kidnapped its young women,
hacked the right feet from its warrior men.

Mother worked for Spanish in the Schools
but couldn't hear the Navajo presence
—Diné today—Keres or Tewa:
languages of the 19 pueblos
resisting up and down this valley we shared.

Dad made friends with a man from Santa Clara
and we visited one weekend,
ate watermelon on his broken porch
and I replaced the images from a childhood book
with real outdoor ovens, real children staring back.

Much later the casinos brought jobs and schools
profit long denied,
a laptop for every family at Sandia:
gaming with its welcome cash
and baffled dreams.

Fast forward half a century, Albuquerque reaches
for a million, flaunts air base and university,
a Federal Court House
that lined the pockets of a few,
old families and their newer neighbors.

Hispanics and Indians speak louder now, African Americans
no longer only work the trains that brought them west.
Like other towns, lesser histories unfold,
lesser mayors stoke political futures
and tomorrow's whatever-centennials
may one day celebrate the protests of today.

La Placita, Old Town, 2009

Words I'd never heard took up residence
in my mouth.
Montaño, even if city signage
refused to put the tilda over the n,

names like *De Vargas, Cabeza de Vaca*
or *Juan Tabó*,
shepherds and assassins enshrined on street corners
unquestioned and mispronounced.

Indian words like *Acoma, Navajo*—now *Diné*—
or place names like *Canyon de Chelly*
the conquerors left us with
when they couldn't speak what they couldn't hear.

Names imposed: *Oñate, Coronado, Santa Fe.*
Another's holy faith bringing death
and leaving division, delighting
those who arrive on private planes.

Common words like *tijeras* and *frijoles,*
scissors and beans
began to quiver on my tongue,
stood easily in later years.

I too came from somewhere else,
a childhood far away,
with other sounds in my ears,
other familiars in my mouth.

The new words tested teeth, stretched lips
and exercised my landscape
until language caught meaning in its net
and I knew nothing was what it pretended.

Community Center, Buena Vista & Coal, 2009

Friday Night at the Community Center

The street is *Buena Vista,* Good View,
but the corner building
sheds its peeling stucco
of fake adobe,
scuffed walls sweat the used up sound
of old 78s.

Friday night at the Community Center
our fathers shuttled us there
to stand and yearn:
stuffed bras, cinched waists,
shifting
from foot to foot.

I always stood against the wall
where girls no one asked to dance
watched our popular classmates
stomp across the wooden floor
obedient eyes lost in strains
of repetitious sound.

Crinolines. Circle skirts.
Diminishing hope
then home to bed
with a photo of the basketball team
pressed against future promise
of breasts.

Kissing his face in that picture
was the closest I got to junior high romance
until an older dropout asked me out

and I gagged on his tongue
pumping machine-gun fire
down my throat.

I don't know when the Community Center
closed its doors,
its western music beat gone still,
ferocity of spring winds
whipping sharp nettle of tumbleweed
across a cracked patio.

I turn a corner. The old building
greets me:
hungry, mocking,
vomiting memory
too sad and hapless to forget,
too smoldering in pain.

If only we could do it over again. If we
could do it over
with what we know now:
a different music,
other rules or no rules
but pure rhythm of the human heart.

When emphysema finally took me from the darkroom I'd inhabited thirty years, I couldn't let go of one small tool of the trade. It's called a grain-finder, elegant little black metal stand with precision magnifying glass and mirror. You slide your negative into the enlarger's neg holder and position the small device on the piece of photo paper waiting to receive its blast of light. Placing one eye over the magnifying glass, you can see the negative's grain and adjust the lens so that each dot stands brilliantly apart from the next, assuring a perfectly focused print.

I knew I would never use this tool again, yet couldn't bring myself to let it go. It's so perfect, I told myself, its weight so at home in the cup of my palm, I couldn't send it off with all the other instruments and tools. One day I might find a young photographer who would like to have it. Then I would give it to her. But so few do film photography anymore.

That grain finder reminds me of my father's metronome. My parents have been gone now long enough so their separate absences are places with personalities of their own: a canyon trail or long sandy beach. Dad died in 1994, Mother in 2006. My brother took the oriental rugs and some of the dark heavy furniture, sold many of the things none of us liked, always making sure to divide what he got among the siblings. My sister wanted the beautiful old copper kettles and pots. I took one small Navajo rug and a large plant I was able to keep alive a few brief years. The one object I longed to have but never found was our father's metronome.

As a child I would fall asleep to its rhythms. When Dad practiced his 'cello, the sound of the pyramid-shaped device found a deeper place in me than the musical notes. I remember asking what it was, a question vying in significance with those about why the planets don't fall from the sky or what makes a traffic light change from red to green. And I remember my father's response. In his gentle voice he explained that it kept a musician's time.

It certainly didn't keep that time perfectly. As it aged, a momentary slowdown might shift the rhythm slightly. Dad aged too, and didn't seem to notice. The polished case was rich mahogany, wood that has held special meaning for me since. A tiny metal hook secured its front cover; unlatching that hook revealed a vertical scale of little cross-lines with fractional numbers. Another piece released the rod with a metal weight which then moved back and forth, when it worked well tapping a rhythm determined by its position on the rod: near the bottom a rapid count; as it rose a slower beat.

I am my family's musical misfit, its one member never successful at any instrument. They said my sister was a natural; she moved from half-sized violin to piano, and later played the guitar and sang. My brother still enjoys his viola, attending summer music camps and occasionally organizing chamber music sessions with friends. From childhood on, I tried. First the piano, taught by an aunt in distant memory. Then, when we moved to New Mexico, accordion with elderly Mr. Berg. At my first and only recital I couldn't remember how to end the piece, and kept going back to the beginning until I fled the stage in tears. A little black plastic third grade tonette, blown in group anonymity, may have been my only success. That year my public school music teacher singled me out on the playground and tried to make me sing the scales before a gathering of jeering students. I opened my mouth but no sound came. When I wet my pants and ran home from that playground, her vain entreaties still echoing in my ears, it should have sent a message to my parents that music and I spelled trauma. This incident gave birth to their assertion that sadly I, their oldest daughter, was tone deaf.

They never again insisted I take music lessons. I was the one who asked, believing one instrument after another might be the one. Until the last when—young woman just out of a first bad marriage—I asked my father if he would teach me the 'cello. It might have been about spending time together. Our Sunday morning lessons were painful, especially for him. I'd practice determinedly, but it was hardly a match. My fingers on the strings never seemed to find anything approaching the right spot. I would draw my bow, curving my wrist just so, but the sounds that issued forth could only be described as harrowing. At the end of one patient year my father suggested I might want to try piano, or some other instrument on which the notes were more precisely located.

But this is not only about my failure at music. Mostly it's about my father's metronome. When an old-fashioned non-digital model like his appeared on the television screen the other night, my body went limp in memory. Once again I saw the rod swing back and forth and heard its steady beat. There was even a whiff of Dad's Old Spice and pipe tobacco. For a few moments he was with me again, cradling me in his arms.

Old Bordelon

Old Bordelon, Cajun transplant to my childhood neighborhood
brought Kosher meat from Denver
on his weekly trucker's run.

His wife and seven daughters all redheads but an eighth,
the longed-for son,
was born with his father's straight black hair.

Today every Albuquerque supermarket has its Kosher shelf,
Latin and Asian specialties
claim whole aisles.

I still remember wetting my pants the day the old man
chased me around their yard,
a roaring blow torch in his hand,

embarrassed crack of his oldest daughter's laugh,
her mother's quivering smile,
the rich colors

of the great Oriental rug the family gave Our Lady of Fatima
parish hall,
a tithe the size of a football field.

Perfect Is Always What I Saw

Old voices sound along this block of patient homes
their puffed-out teenage chests
ordinary front yards now,
single-car garages, sagging mail boxes.

Your flute-like voice still grounds
our high school friendship:
a tone I never mastered.
Your father still slurs his after dinner scotch,
still smells of Republican politics, refined abuse.

But it's your mother's welcome draws me
each time I pass your childhood home,
turn my eyes
to catch a narrow glimpse of the windows
where Kleenex and matching toilet paper
kept their pastel watch.

Her broad girth promised cookies, comfort,
heritage of eastern money,
family in perfect harmony.
Perfect is always what I saw
and you were steadfast, never revealing
a crack in the façade.

Until, forty years into an awkward future
we spoke freely
of drunken fathers and frightened mothers,
what the pale yellow or lime green tissue
masked or wiped from sight.

By then you were long free of your own
Hungarian knight,
click of his menacing heels.
The breast cancer that would end your life
still cowered beyond ambiguity
of medical scans.

You told me your father didn't leave,
it was your gentle mother
finally threw him out.
He gone now decades from your life
and his. She living longer but also dead.

At the end you would cherish the joy
you deserved
with a man who had eyes
to see your weave of colored yarns
and painter's heart,
a man who could be lover and best friend
before you died.

Today when I round the corner
of your childhood block
and hear those voices that rise and call
I listen for your mother's quiet tones
just before she took her spent life back,
giving you permission to live
what was left of yours.

The Sunshine, Kimo and El Rey stood in downtown majesty, crowning our Saturday afternoons with all we desired: Esther Williams and her perfect water syncopation. Shelley Winters' alluring lisp. Ginger Rogers and Fred Astaire in exquisite harmony. Elizabeth Taylor and her stallion; even in black and white her eyes were violet blue. Debbie Reynolds. Burt Lancaster. Montgomery Clift.

Paris was where we wanted to dance—in the rain of course—or on a South Pacific beach, wet bodies clinging to our man's while the drama of far-off war sounded through flutter of royal palms.

Our female idols all had 18-inch waists and tiny turned up noses. Eyes downcast, then slowly raised to melt into those of the man she loved. We could feel our teenage lips pressed against that man's. No tongues yet. Lips were as wickedly delicious as our imaginations could endure.

My weekly allowance just covered the price of the under-12 ticket plus one small bag of M & Ms. Sometimes I'd buy a Mounds Bar instead; its gritty mix of coconut and dark chocolate still lures me.

At the uptown Lobo, depending on mood and finances, I'd alternate between sticking my flat chest out—pretending I needed adult admission—and trying to get in for the junior price. Each had its advantage.

After the show our lustful dreams propelled us weak-kneed from the theater, fully inhabiting Debbie or Elizabeth. I remember wondering if some sort of biological metamorphosis might actually have taken place during those two hours of movie house dark, such was the intensity of the changes in body and state of mind. For hours we were our idols.

If we'd known those men were gay our world would have spun into distant space, our longing altered forever.

Sixty years later the Sunshine and El Rey host second-rate cowboy bands. The Lobo's triangular marquee announces the weekly services of a religious congregation called City on a Hill. Only the Kimo has kept and nurtures its old elegance; light still glows mysterious behind the carved masks that flank its stage. Now some of the great women singer/songwriters perform there when they come to town.

Ours was an era that offered equal measure of innocence and ignorance. Back in the 1950s, by the time we'd turned our attention to Ingrid Bergman everything had changed.

Downtown Albuquerque, Kimo Theater, 2009

Before Sputnik

Perkins taught English, diagramed endless sentences
on the board, once made me stay after
for passing a note in class,
no neck between round head and padded chest,
reveling in authority.

Shannon was Drama, lent me her wedding dress
for my starring role in our senior play,
said she'd only been married days,
her alcohol breath
no cause for rebuke back then.

Biology's V'Cella gave me a generous D, after all
he rented a room from Mom and Dad.
In the microscope I drew my own eye
over and over,
its lashes a growth of curled worms.

Tiny Videla barked instructions across the court,
still evoked gym teacher fantasies
at our fortieth class reunion.
The following year her obituary
brought a stab of pain.

They're all gone now, even Erhard: casual sponsor
of yearbook and student paper,
my favorite until the day
he took me aside and described his penis
in less than literary terms.

There were others. But Perkins, Shannon,
V'Cella, Videla and Erhard
are those I remember from
my pre-Sputnik high school years
when girls weren't encouraged in math or science

like after 1957. The Reds had beaten us into space
and our government finally acknowledged
it needed our minds
to compete, compete,
compete.

I Was Alone That Night

When I was a child the desert bloomed
right down to Highland High
our white kids' school
on the eastern edge of town.
Fierce winds whipped sand
to the backs of our calves
sharp sting against young skin.

Cholla and Prickly Pear, stout Barrel cacti
their sudden flowers
met us long before those mountains
rose in blue distance,
watermelon light each afternoon.

Highland for the families who arrived
from somewhere else
and settled in the heights.
Albuquerque High for the tough kids:
New Mexican, Mexican American,
Black sons and daughters
of the Atchison Topeka & Santa Fe
or off-reservation Indians come to town
in search of work.
Chicano, African or Native American
weren't words we had back then.
Only assimilation, The American Dream
enforced unevenly.

Some girls said Albuquerque High boys
kissed better
and when the captain of the downtown football team

asked me out I trembled yes
beneath anxious folds
of Dotted Swiss.

When one running-back hand tore at my blouse
and the other charged between my legs
I cried for him to stop
and to the couple in front for help.
Their moans sounded light years away.
He laughed, pried deeper, at ease
with male right.

Through the triangle of window
a splash of stars
seemed distant and pale.
I took remembered advice
and brought my knee up
fast and sharp to his groin.

He let go and I pushed the door,
leapt free and ran
down a rocky road
'til I hit pavement
and kept on running
afraid he might follow.

But I was alone that night
flying toward city lights
panting and crying
slowing to walk
then running again
until my house appeared.

Years later I could say
the word rape

—what the high school football star
did to me that night—
know he didn't follow
because it wasn't me he wanted,

only conquest there on that car seat
in the presence of buddies,
only the ancient ritual
of male entitlement:
another notch
on the stock of his teenage gun.

Albuquerque High School, 1947
Photo courtesy Albuquerque Museum

Decreasing the Property Values

On the street of my high school angst
just at the corner
where Creative Writing's house
decreased the property values
—bringing the whole neighborhood down—
my teacher took me aside one day
and told me his penis was thin but long
like a pencil.

I made a sharp left and kept on walking.
Property values were in the news.
My parents mentioned them
when explaining why they couldn't rent
to my friend, the student from Ghana,
rejected all over our neighborly town
for too different, too black.

The way it was. Called normal
by almost everyone.

The Sorting Hat

Last night when you exited stage right
your sad eyes lingered in my dream,
the grace your body held
beneath its matching sweater set,
ethereal stance.

Perhaps wondering if we knew and of course
we didn't,
couldn't place such delicate accent,
imagine the secret you hid
behind your studied silence.

Miss Shannon pronounced you perfect
for our senior play,
no audition
and you spoke your lines
with natural grace,

moved ghostlike, lifting the script
out of high school make-believe
to memories
none of us possessed.
Born to act, we conceded grudgingly.

No one said friend or invited you home,
did more than notice faint lines
at the corners of your eyes
or pulling down
your mouth.

Not only the evidence in flesh
but how you moved
your arms and legs,
used space
inhabited time.

You were different and different unsettled us.
Now I wonder: a breakdown
before it was okay
to hurt in mind
as well as body,

or back from the place they sent young girls,
forced to give your baby
to proper parents
before you could feel her skin
against your cheek?

What happened to the rest of your life
after the sorting hat
stopped building righteous walls
between the good girls
and the bad?

I Google without response, want
to tell you time can circle back
and now that it's too late
some of us are old enough
to welcome the woman you were then.

This Could Have Happened

When the dog of invasion
bit my shoulder
I hardly felt his teeth.

It's his wild lunge and growl
still embedded in that tissue
of memory

behind my eyes,
the animal sound
of canines ripping flesh.

This could have happened
at the corner of 4th and Central
or where desert gathers

its sandy folds
against the mountain's face.
The place no longer holds

its coordinates
and so I wake each night
from a fever of battered dream.

Until There Were No More Bottle Caps

It was never the town, even when rooms and sidewalks
mattered enough to wrinkle my dreams.
It was always the land: that desert light,
mountains drawing me
into their crevices, landswept points on a map
of time and storyline.

All through school, in spite of cheerleader lure
or homecoming court, my treasure
was a store of Geological Survey maps,
unwieldy heft rolled beneath my bed,
fine lines
pulling me over rises and hollows
to that secret space.

I couldn't make peace with my parents' lies
but lied to them to cover my tracks,
said I was with a girlfriend,
let the girlfriend wonder about a boy,
drove, then stopped and parked
along a country road,
set out from that parked car
like Livingston or Shackleton
—names I only vaguely knew—
followed those delicate lines
across small hills, into valleys
beyond rocks as imposing as any African kopje

until there were no more bottle caps, no fisted wads
of crumpled paper, nothing
smelling of civilization,

how we were taught its implacable progress,
learned to build our lives
submissive to its appetites.

I turned a corner, shunned all that was packaged
and ready, sought a time before,
always before,
then slowly removed each constraint
of clothing: blouse, skirt, petticoat,
folded each sock

and lifted my naked body onto sun-soaked rock,
settled flesh and racing heart
freeing them to dream of a time before,
always before,
when Conquest rose in future tense
and alone meant alone.

Once the journey began
I knew I might fly further back
to a point no longer elusive,
spend the night
before the arrival of humans.

Nothing spoke to me then
but heat and wind
caressing my skin
like a serving at table,
filling me as no other meal could.

Those visits taught me alone doesn't have
to be lonely, brought me
to syllables I've finally begun to shape
on the road out.

Back then I still traveled the road in
and all I had were directions
on a dollar map.

It was never the town itself but the hues
of space and light
moving out from its measured grid,
impossible rainbows, supplications
to an anti-God
sometimes willing to hold my hand
when answers confused my need to know.

Back then I had no choice but lie
to keep my date with possibility,
couldn't know years later
I'd climb the four-thousand-foot trail
foothill to crest, desert to timber,
rockslide and beyond.

Back then I couldn't envision a future
of no one but me in the canyon,
no human breath or voice
but the peregrine falcon, rattler,
cottontail or whitetail deer, black bear
sometimes lumbering down
or single coyote forever ahead of the pack.

Adventure was self-contained back then,
event not journey,
end not waypoint to the bridge
my life would become:
a feedback loop
still leading me out
from this desert city of my youth
and back through its surrogate streets.

Volcano and Mesa, 2009

Two Deaths

Swimming at the A one summer morning,
public pool where neighbors gathered
and no one admitted
relaxing their bladder
a safe distance
from others doing the same,
I looked up
just as a plane
rising or descending above the airport
exploded into a ball of flame.

Flights didn't fill the sky
in tens of thousands then
so accidents weren't common
and those who saw the apocalypse
stood this side of a pumice wall
unable to shape the words
that described mute horror
or vicarious thrill.

When I think of the A pool I remember
a family we knew back then:
mother, father, daughters and a son,
a family not unlike ours
except the son grew up
to be a brilliant dancer
whose father pretended he wasn't
one of them.

Forty years later a football field
worth of AIDS quilt
came to town

and I saw his mother again
lovingly patting her son's square.
I thought of that ball of fire in the sky,
two sorts of death:
the first without reason or meaning,
the second crowning a lonely life
of identity and art.

Road to volcano cones, 2009

Gay Meant Have a Good Time

We didn't know it then but the three of us
would end up loving our own,
didn't know about same-sex love,
the word homosexual
still hid in medical texts
and gay meant have a good time.

Or maybe they knew. I didn't and would marry
more than my share of men,
enter middle age
before I could love a woman
while they, two young queers
in those stifling fifties,
chose silence over certain death.

Three high school misfits
with nothing to do
but drive the rutted earth
of Albuquerque's West Mesa
one night,
hauling a truck bed of old tires
to the largest volcano's shadowy crater.

Those tires, a couple cans of kerosene
and matches were all we needed.
The fire burned quickly
but smoke billowed high
in predawn light
as we raced home to hug one another
and listened to the radio
implore our city to evacuate.

We pricked our fingers, mixed our blood
to seal the promise
we'd never tell
and for years we didn't.
Clarence, kleptomaniac
turned antique dealer in Bernalillo,
died in his fifties.

James showed up at our high school's fortieth
too nervous to stand
with my partner and me.
He'd come all the way from England,
won the prize for traveling farthest
though how far he lived
from his own volcano
few of the other aging boys and girls
could know.

Looking west I always think of that night:
luminous dare
of my teenage years
when for moments our city leaders
thought Vesuvius
and I learned to keep a secret.

What I saw was Mother in her hospital bed, emerging from sleep to Dad's and my prepared smiles. Ann and Johnny were too young to visit. We'd left them in the parking lot from where they'd promised to wave up to her window when one of us signaled. I'd practiced staying upbeat, not crying.

What my mother saw were our faces, whatever each struggled with beneath its careful mask, floating in a post-anesthesia haze.

What Mother heard when she woke was the doctor telling her they'd removed her left breast as well as the lymph nodes under her arm. No more, no less. I had met this surgeon with his local "best in the business" fame, and thought him distant and surly. Today I would add pretentious.

Cancer happened to Mother in 1954. Authority was to be respected, and the word not uttered anywhere at any time.

What I wore at my mother's bedside was my favorite gray gingham dress. The one with the scoop neck half filled with horizontal tucks, suggesting cleavage where none existed.

While the woman who gave me life and nursed me through my first months contemplated the loss of this body part and looming death, I did my nightly exercises: bringing arms to chest level, down-turned fingers almost touching and elbows at right angles, jerking them back and forth like a fledgling bird. I'd been told this would make my breasts bigger, which at that point meant noticeable.

What Mother wore was a humiliating hospital gown over a large white bandage and assortment of drainage tubes. Beneath her forced smile she wore defeat.

A week later we brought her home. Lovingly Dad tried to clean the wound, but fainted during his first attempt. That's when I took over. Our father, courageous in all the ways that count, was dizzied by ordinary medical procedures, the drawing of blood. A congenital trait, people said. His response to Mother's loss was a physical tic, but she read it as rejection. From then on they slept in separate rooms. I don't know if she ever allowed him near her again.

Sixty years ago, in my family's culture, cancer equaled shame. The fear of loosing our mother doesn't rise nearly as large in memory as the public silence around the word, or her efforts to deflect people's sense of her as someone damaged by the disease, a woman less than whole.

Twice daily, for the rest of her long life, she wound an ace bandage the length of her swollen arm. For the first ten or fifteen years, when friends or acquaintances asked about that bandage she told them she had twisted her arm driving. When I wondered out loud one day if she thought they believed the story, she said no, she supposed not; but continued telling it.

Such was the social dread of mere association with cancer. Before questions and the right to make up your own mind. Before Betty Ford. Before the American Cancer Association's national campaigns. Before pink ribbons and speaking out and women supporting women. Before new research—at least some of it aimed at prevention and a cure. Before reconstructive surgery and a women's movement that encouraged us to believe we are worth more than the sum of our parts.

From then on, everything in Mother's life was measured by concavity, scar tissue and a word that couldn't be spoken. I try to imagine the texture of her shame, and rage at my inability to help her through. Albuquerque held the silence. Our family held it. Silence was currency.

My mother inhabited that silence, but she also lived: among the fortunate in a time when such a statistic was hard to come by.

Years before, as a very young child lying across my parents' bed one afternoon, I had watched Mother coming from her bath. Naked above the waist, her perfect breasts moved slightly as she walked. Their rich brown nipples still swing gently back and forth whenever I hear the word cancer, spoken freely now.

Have Some Dessert

Ellie Randall Spaghetti smothered
overcooked pasta and ground round
with a two-pound brick of Velveeta
melted and burnt to a darkened crust on top.

After moving west she added a bowl of chile
to her repertoire: sweet green pepper
and onions, canned black olives
and reliable hamburger

with a can of pinto beans
and red chile powder on the side,
everyone serving
their own preference for heat.

Few at our table knew the meat
was horse instead of beef.
Bloody eggs and powdered milk
brought Mother the satisfaction

of saving a few cents here, a dollar there.
She always willing
to explain how it added up,
Dad beaming at her reliable thrift.

My childhood predated the anorexic angst
burdening later generations,
diets and other fads were novelties to us.
In high school

I could always take ten pounds off
despite the ritual milkshakes

at the soda fountain down the street.
Chocolate is still my flavor.

But as I grew the pounds increased
imperceptibly, exponentially:
my armor against Grandpa's abuse
catching up fast.

My 98-pound mother always boasted:
Look how much I eat,
never gained an ounce,
claimed her perfect figure a matter of will
while urging me, always urging me:
Have some dessert.

Above the Colors of a Dirndl Skirt

She was a big woman, heavy breasts
filling peasant blouse
above the colors of a dirndl skirt.
Today she would use pants
but we all wore skirts back then
cinching our yearning waists
to a lying destiny.

I never knew if she was my parents' friend
or mine:
she and her husband,
artists with a couple of toddling kids.
Memory no longer assigns
a measure of generations.

Alice and Jack. Jack and Alice,
university couple
painting and shaping clay,
asking questions
beyond my awkward reach,
trundling their little ones behind.

Until one day Alice was sick and no one
could name the illness
come to claim those breasts,
open and close her hands,
whispered hospital stay,
relieved homecoming,
sudden death.

No one knew. No one could say.
Silence floods drifting images
as those voices rise once more
in make-believe phrases
like "she was just beginning to make it"
or "what a shame."

I left town.
Alice's shattered family stayed.
Jack visited us in Mexico
huddled on our stoop
a bottle of beer in his deflated hand.

Years later I came home to search
for the murals my parents said
graced every floor
of the First National Bank Building:
success too late
in a life cut short.

I went with a friend, announced
we wanted to see
the walls I'd imagined for years:
paint dripping from Alice's brushes
pure color coming home.

The receptionist's blank smile told us
there were no murals
in this building,
"Sorry," she said. "I should know,
I've worked here for years."

Images painted over
like my town's beautiful family
overcome by the picture-perfect demands

of a decade dripping hypocrisy,
rancid silence and lies
when even art
couldn't beat the odds.

Petroglyph National Park, west of Albuquerque, 2009

Swaying Left

Along a dirt road high on the Río Grande bluff
a low adobe house urged us forward,
my lover promising its writer of modest fame
would prove a gracious host.

Writer and wife cared for Coronado Monument;
ancient ruin bearing the insult of its Spanish name
but alive with the paintings
of those who lived there centuries before.

They welcomed us to spend the night
in their warm shed. I cannot remember
why we didn't drive back to Albuquerque,
twenty miles if that.

It was the woman who claimed my heart that night.
One-armed, she told us it was hard
walking back from Bernalillo
balancing groceries against a spring wind.

The lover who brought me there has been gone
for decades, those caretakers dead as well.
Coronado's Monument now crowns its bluff
with museum and paid staff.

Closing my eyes I see a phantom woman
swaying left to balance her lost arm,
struggling along a road now paved,
bringing food to her man who writes at home.

Kiva, Coronado State Monument, 2009

Favorite Places

Dad's favorite place was the loop trail
behind their last house
where he walked each day
his German Shepherd
by his side.

Later it was The Pit where he cheered
Friday night basketball
alone or with friends.
Our mother hated sports.

Always the Lobo men.
"The women
just don't play as well," he said,
a preference I never could undo.

Mother's favorite place was the university
where she flirted with professors,
took every class twice
and favored perfection over use.

My baby brother John: Johnny Boy or JB
to distinguish him from Dad,
went to banks
when he was eight or nine.

He'd trade a few bills for coins
—pennies, nickels, quarters—
examine each one
for the collection that grew
with him.

Our sister Ann must have had
her favorite places too
but I never knew her well enough
to discover where they were.

Jefferson Junior High, 1947
Photo commissioned by the First National Bank
for promotional material.
Photo courtesy Albuquerque Museum.

Send Coyote Down

Through windows, car windows and the windows
of our home, I looked at the world,
measured its distance
absorbed picture post card wisdom:
no kind of wisdom at all.

In gym class I always had a doctor's note,
forgery good enough
to fool teachers who didn't care,
as I tried to avoid being the last one picked
by every team.

Four thousand feet above my town
great mountains rise to the east,
craggy elevations where deer, black bear
and mountain sheep send Coyote down
to see how the city folk are doing.

North and south the stone walls
of ancient communities
carve their own horizons
among the piñon, sage and arroyo beds
bringing sustenance in earlier times.

To the west dead volcanoes, gorges and desert
spread all the way to California, a distance
I once drove 18 hours straight,
absorbing the land through open windows,
no air conditioning then.

Half a century later, when I returned to my town
to hike and bike and climb my mountain

(it took me a year and a half to get to the top)
I found the wisdom of land
where it always was

patient, lying in wait for the woman
who still wonders why
she never stepped outside
all those years ago
when connection hid its face.

Weapon of Mass Destruction 1

Dry heaves sucked air from sky
but only for seconds,
we'd look up, then at one another,
astonishment mixed with hometown pride
as if to say: isn't it something—
acknowledging life
abetted by new technology
breaking the barrier of sound.

No one protested those sudden jolts
to consciousness and breath,
no one extrapolated beyond our own ear drums
vibrating high above familiar range,
at least no one we knew,
no one they hadn't taken away somewhere
and hidden behind a veil
of see no, hear no, speak no evil.

At Los Alamos they were building
a weapon of mass destruction
with Hiroshima and Nagasaki in the cross hairs.
Oppenheimer and his crew
planted their promise of vaporizing death
in the cedar-scented forests of northern New Mexico.
Japanese children, skin soft as children's everywhere,
marked for the agony to come.

In the off-limits neighborhood
we called The Base
fighter planes lifted into the sky
then roared back to earth

tearing at the rhythm of our breath
like Gulliver's hammer on Lilliput Island.
Hometown pride garbled the questions
some of us would ask
as we grew to our own sad certainty.

When my mother's hair fell out
she said
it must have been the things they did back then.

Weapon of Mass Destruction 2

Hiroshima: alive one day—a couple about to wed,
the family sitting at grandmother's bedside,
homes and public gardens,
their little curved bridges and pristine trees.
In less than a minute
heat like the sun exploding
sucks air from air, flesh and flowers and song:
all silent.

Two days later Nagasaki also disappears,
footnote to hearts split open
from Hanoi to Havana, Cape Town to Berlin.
Still, for those in that second city
skin melts to bone,
before and after rises stark, cuts as deep,
sounds as tortured in echoing ears.

In Albuquerque: two hours south of the cluster of labs
hidden among New Mexico's pungent forests,
not much farther north of Alamogordo's test site
where the bomb to end all wars
was introduced as Trinity: a three in one
of secrecy, deception and death,

all we got was the lie about preemption saving lives,
ending a war already won,
and the lonely pilot of a plane carrying infamy
whose memoir sold out
because the story of one white man makes better news
than two hundred thousand foreign dead.

Lovelace Hospital, 1953. Intersection of Ridgecrest & Gibson Blvds. Photo courtesy Albuquerque Museum.

Lovelace Hospital sits like an aging hulk, high in Albuquerque's southeast heights. Once a famed research institution, now an HMO bought out by one management company after another, until local lore warns against spending any time in its emergency unit unless you're prepared to get sicker than when you arrived. In my early twenties I visited a pale young psychiatrist there, the sessions paid for by my job at the time. What I remember was the doctor's faintly smug smile and impassive demeanor, unchanged even when I took the small polished wood figure of a dove from a table and threw it as hard as I could at his large plate glass window. That window framed an imposing view of the Sandia Mountains to the east. The dove didn't make a dent.

I wouldn't have suspected what was going on at Lovelace then. In the early 1960s thirteen women—working airplane pilots, maintenance specialists, flight instructors, some of them among the first Army WASPS*—were secretly tested there. The Soviets had beaten us into space and threatened to retain supremacy in exploring that "last frontier." In his commanding Cold War voice President Kennedy challenged the country to send a man to the moon by the end of the decade. Randolph Lovelace was the chairman of NASA's Life Sciences Committee. Against prevailing prejudice, he along with a very few other men believed women should be considered as astronauts.

The nation's space program knew the women's smaller, lighter bodies would be costeffective in zero gravity; they would need less oxygen and take up less room in a spacecraft, saving nearly $1,000 a pound. And so it let Jerrie Cobb and the others believe they had a shot at participation. The women endured months of grueling tests, including hours in the total darkness

* Women Air Force Service Pilots, active during World War II.

and silence of an isolation tank, pain tolerance measured by how long they could keep their hands in ice, freezing water injected into their inner ears, three feet of rubber hose snaked down their throats, drinking radioactive water, and endless psychological quizzes—the same taken by the Mercury 7 men but in an era in which "girls" were patronized and belittled even more than we are today. The women knew they couldn't show pain, fear, even discomfort. Perhaps inspired by the model of perfect female helpmeet, they kept their fixed smiles through it all. All thirteen passed the astronaut tests and, the Lovelace doctors conceded, with fewer complaints than the men.

Throughout the first half of 1961, across the street from Lovelace Hospital, these brave, talented and hopeful women stayed at the Bird of Paradise Motel, dilapidated even then. Up each morning at five to begin another day of tests. Back each evening to laugh with one another and wonder how their male counterparts were holding up. These women had temporarily left husbands and children, quit jobs, risked everything for a chance they believed was real. But after they'd all passed the tests, in August of that year the bad news came, sudden and blunt: Lovelace's "regret to advise." NASA had the data it needed and stereotypical bias proved too powerful an obstacle to the women's participation.

Over the next years there were letters, pleas, protest marches, Senate hearings; Jerrie Cobb even met with Vice President Lyndon Johnson. Never one to say anything bad about anyone, she didn't reveal the contents of their conversation until 2007. Only then did she admit the Vice President had looked at her and said: "Jerrie, if we let you or other women into the space program, we'd have to let blacks in. We'd have to let Mexican Americans in, and Chinese Americans. We'd have to let every minority in, and we just can't do it."

Buzz Aldrin. Neil Armstrong. Michael Collins. Alan B. Shepard, Jr. John Glenn. These and others were household names belonging to the men who had "the right stuff." Two of them took "one giant leap for mankind" in July of 1969. And the male parade continued to engage in dozens of other space flights: some tragic, all heroic.

Like almost everyone old enough, I remember every astonishing detail of Apollo 11's mission. I had suffered a political repression following the 1968 Student Movement and was in hiding in Mexico City at the time. But even those grim circumstances couldn't keep me from sitting breathless before a small black and white TV, compelled by images hard to believe were real: it was July 20, 1969 and a man was walking on the moon.

Not long after the fabled landing, a young Nicaraguan poet named Leonel Rugama wrote "The Earth is a Satellite of the Moon," a poem in which he juxtaposed the Apollo flights with his country's excruciating poverty. The magna event affected different people in different ways. Many believed space exploration would continue full speed ahead, that Mars would be next and—who knew—the colonization of other planets. The same voracious sense of conquest so pervasive on earth extended beyond its confines. A few judged the moon landing a hoax. Even as I marveled at the exploration of space, I wondered why we were spending so many billions on such endeavors while poverty on earth affected so many. For me the convergence—my time underground and a man walking on the moon—belongs to a deeper story, not for these pages.

Jerrie Cobb. Gene Nora Stumbough. Bernice Steadman. Sarah Gorelick. Jane Hart. Irene Leverton. Rhea Hurtle. Wally Funk. Myrtle Cagle. Jan and Marion Dietrich, who were twins. Their names never became household words. Today they sound a litany of betrayal. These and others were the women who believed their government was acting in good faith when it tested them like the men. All were sent home without apology when those in power rejected the idea of women in space.

Thirty-eight years after their profound disappointment, the survivors watched Sally Ride, Eileen Collins and several other women fly beyond earth's atmosphere. In July, 1999, when Collins became the first woman space shuttle Commander, she made sure her foremothers who'd dreamed high and endured that rigorous testing so many years before had places of honor near the launching pad. Like women throughout time, Jerrie Cobb and her sisters had been promised the stars, lied to, used, humiliated and, when no longer useful, tossed aside. Even today's female members of the space program are referred to as women astronauts while the men are astronauts without the adjective.

The Bird of Paradise Motel is gone. Lovelace still stands, shabby and only partially used, although its research component continues to operate. Secret experiments are almost never engineered for the common good, to feed or clothe or bring peace. Who knows what experiments may be taking place there now?

The information for this piece comes from a variety of news sources beyond my own experience. I am particularly indebted to Almost Astronauts: 13 Women Who Dared to Dream by Tanya Lee Stone, Candlewick Press, Somerville, Massachusetts, 2009.

Where We Were

Six friends at a round wooden table bring the Canal
into perfect focus. Suez 1956,
first threat of an oil war
and the fall of European colonialism.
That night sucked breath from our bodies,
our certainty the world would end.

Don and Valerie and others I've forgotten
juggled before and after.
Three years earlier Korea jolted us
from complacency
before nuclear arms, Vietnam and subsequent crises
would bludgeon our immortality.

Suez was first. Albuquerque at that round wooden table,
earliest remembered notion of where we were
and how afraid.

Theater of the Absurd

Art model, insurance agency receptionist,
writer of manuals for the Redstone Missile
among my early Albuquerque jobs,
the manuals written for sixth-graders:
maintenance and operations alike.

In that theater of the absurd
I had top-secret clearance,
props that included padlocked trashcans
where typewriter ribbons went to die
after a single use.

When I moved on to become a writer
in New York
my old boss called one night:
could I get a young colleague an abortion,
sure I was up to the task.

Asking around I ended up with Dr. Ann,
a hotel on upper Broadway,
her shabby waiting room
filled with other scared young women,
frozen in blood-soaked shame.

In nineteen-fifty-eight you could go
to a home for unwed mothers,
relinquish your baby to proper parents
or bleed to death in exchange for $800
payable upfront.

My ex-boss's secretary never said
he got her pregnant,
and she didn't die.
All I got was a heartfelt thank you
back when Roe vs. Wade
was as distant as it is fragile now.

More than fifteen thousand figures etched
by the ancients in this broad canyon
cover dark volcanic rock
at city's edge:
horned masks,

mountain lion trailing a snake behind one ear
and birds: one whose beak
extends to circle its floating perch
where message still rides the energy of time
and image bores through memory.

No tree or any other shade, only the ragged
rises and dips along a powdery path
hugging the shattered hillside,
our route surprised by a yellow cactus bloom
or desert lizard panting through the sage.

Volcanic boulders tumble this western escarpment
chipped to rust red beneath a polished surface,
line of craters above
and down below the grasses
growing through old lava.

You dub one image Big Head, what you also call
yourself: large square face, forehead
bearing one vertical worry line,
ears and legs and stand-up hair
protruding straight from bodiless stance.

Here a tight spiral may depict the supernova
startling these skies in 1054,
signify gathering place or starting point.
Shamanic figures
may or may not be shamans.

We have no record of how the people dressed,
what language they spoke,
whether theirs was art or signage,
a gallery left by men and women at work
or children at play.

My Albuquerque childhood knew nothing
of these petroglyphs,
this map destined for their time or ours.
Now law protects the pictures,
requires visitors respect their voice.

But today also brings the encroachment
of development, each new threat
a road will cut this canyon,
giving us yet another grid
of look-alike homes.

The mountain lion and bird, the snake
slithering across its baked surface
bear silent witness, resist.
They speak
and we are well advised to listen.

Alvarado Hotel, 1930. Photo by Wyatt Davis.
Photo Courtesy Albuquerque Museum

Sad Replica

Sad replica of the old Alvarado
stands where trains share their fate
with Greyhound terminal,
red and yellow Rail Runner
carves a new commuter corridor,
homeless men and women
shelter from winter cold
and ghost conversations
filter through the walls.

The old hotel died in 1970,
died no, was murdered
by those who couldn't love
its broad verandahs
where Indians sold their blankets and baskets
to travelers from the east
and Harvey Girls served meals
perfectly timed to the station stop.

Mary Elizabeth Jane Colter,
builder of great hotels
when women weren't yet architects
and the West was still
being won—by men.
No heart for the sounds and smells
of history.

Transportation Center, Downtown Albuquerque, 2009

The Houses Look the Same

The houses look the same:
Tulane Drive northeast
where I bargained a bedroom of my own,
down the hill to Monte Vista Elementary
then up in the other direction
to the junior high where Sammy Wise
yelled elephant snout, leaving me
at odds with my nose
for years.

New in town, Mother made
the Sunday rounds with me,
different church each week,
looking for a youth group that felt right.
Later with my high school date
—the future Baptist preacher—
we discussed the pros and cons of God
perched on a rock at Jémez
after our Senior Prom.

Back when tires went flat and radiators
needed refills, before turn signals
or rearview mirrors,
Dad taught me to drive when I was twelve
—vast ranches
needed their young in pickup trucks—
and I borrowed the family car
for those all-night trips to the desert,
seeking a time before calamity.

Tulane Drive southeast, same number
of blocks south of Central now

as north of the main street then
and sixty years later
my beloved is a woman
still healing from Baptist madness.
All those years needed to learn
religions are dangerous,
churches their sinister traps.

The houses look alike: Pueblo-style
built early in the 1940s
with square stoops,
furnace grates set in oak floors
and little hall shelves
where rotary telephones sat.

Today's telephones have buttons,
compete with cellular models,
Internet, dialup or cable
the communication options
leaving a twentieth century woman
struggling to remember her password
and wondering if password or name
will be etched upon her stone.

It never rained back then
but monsoons soak us now
and something called Xeriscape
has replaced my childhood grass
with gardening more in line
with our efforts to salve
destruction we cannot turn around.

Flames Draw the Heat

Nuggets of deep-fried dough trick hunger,
travel north as a hollow pillow
called sopaipilla: bite a corner,
drip sweet honey into its warm interior
and lick soft edges of crisp dough.

Flour tortillas meet fry bread this side of the Río Grande,
a staple at Pueblo dances, they hold
mutton instead of pork
and satisfy every bit as much
as their cousins to the south.

Tacos and tamales: same name but something else
entirely: Mexican, Tex-Mex, New Mexican:
cuisine as dissimilar
as the cultures that serve them up.

Around here we ask whether green or red
is hotter today
as the metal roasting tumblers spin
and flames draw the heat
from this season's veins and seeds.

An Attitude I Never Learned

—for M.H.

Pure energy exploded the pom-poms she waved
across our high school football field.
It disappeared in a blaze of color, exuberant
leaps and an attitude I never learned.

All I wanted was to be like her, beyond popular:
cheerleader, homecoming attendant,
narrow waist
and eager bounce to her walk.

Her year's queen said goodbye in her wedding dress
from the depths of an early coffin.
Mine also died young
widowing the man she'd loved since thirteen.

Not a block from where we lived my idol's house
hid its perfect secrets,
only a year older
but light years beyond my fingertips.

Decades later, in generational meltdown
her only daughter became a friend,
time a collapsible telescope,
each of us awed by the story's missing half.

Slowly you revealed your childhood's underside:
mother cheerleader's anorexia and prescription pills,
drink and divorce
splitting your life in two.

When you told her of our friendship
she didn't remember me,
but before your mother died
you brought her to one of my readings

and in the restroom, at intermission, told her
I'd written eighty books.
"Well, how thick are they?"
Her question still echoes against the tiles.

We met at Wild Oats Deli. I recognized him by his red satin shirt, broad-brimmed hat and spurs—as unexpected among the arugula and spinach dip as the high school senior exciting my freshman's beating heart half a century before.

Back then he lived with his mother in a trailer park. Mine said how nice she was a Christian Scientist too, thought him handsome and asked if he kissed well. That was Mom: never exactly who you expected beneath the liberal parent guise.

"With his mouth closed," I said (like mother like daughter) which only encouraged her one night to show him how it's done, reducing me to quivering shame, my thundering heart in shambles. Why couldn't my mother play Bridge or serve warm cookies after school?

Now he tells me how proud he was to inherit Red Ryder's name, how he plays the county fairs imparting pure values to the kids, unsure anymore if his name is Dave or Red and answering to both. Then, as shy as all those years ago, he pushes an autographed picture to my side of the table.

When he asks what I've been doing all this time I say writing books. I don't mention my woman lover or the revolution, Cuba, Nicaragua, anything I think might crowd those wide open spaces or startle the rearing steed.

"Me too," he smiles, "I got a couple with aphorisms for the young, helps keep 'em on the straight and narrow. You'd be surprised what tempts kids these days. It's not like back in our time."

I don't say I wouldn't be surprised, but sip my latte as I small-talk this middle-aged cowboy who once pummeled my teenage breath and had me suspended between the right prom corsage and better luck next time.

None of the little stories I pull from our briefly shared past ignite a spark of recognition; he doesn't remember them at all.

"We should do this again," he smiles, and I watch his red satin shoulders lope toward the door, then look down at the 8 x 10 glossy staring up from the table top, sure after all these years we've each made the life we were meant for.

Intersection of Central and Second Street
Taken from second floor of the
Sunshine Building, looking west, 1950.
Photo courtesy of Albuquerque Museum.

Petroglyph National Park, west of Albuquerque, 2009

I am sitting on the ground, near a tree but not leaning against it. I know this because I can see clear blue sky behind my head. A sudden flurry of blackbirds rises off the ground, momentarily obscuring my face, and as it does face and neck disappear. Like a canvass wiped clean of image, only the calm blue sky remains. My bare shoulders show unblemished skin, not a drop of blood. My body from neck down is still there, in its original seated position.

Waking from this dream, I know I must write about Sam Jacobs. Our lives joined briefly in Albuquerque when I was just 18, he a year older. We'd met the summer before, on the S.S. Queen Mary—the original. After high school graduation, my family spent the summer in Europe, sailing on one of the lower decks: tourist accommodations they were called back then, a grade up from steerage. Sam and his family were in first class, but he appeared one night—rich boy's swagger hiding the insecurity always brooding just beneath the surface—and said "Come on, I know how to get us into a wild dance."

I followed the young man who told tales that had me flying. He was from Cincinnati, a wealthy family that kept horses. His father ran a chain of department stores. The year before he had climbed the Matter Horn—I barely knew it was a mountain—and there were few musical instruments he couldn't play. Cincinnati's Black dance clubs and minor league ice hockey were also part of his repertoire. Deftly hidden was his childhood stint at the Menninger Clinic and the oozing rash spilling from inside each elbow beneath a freshly pressed long-sleeved shirt.

I thought I was in love; it would be years before I understood that Sam had been my ticket out, escape from home. In the 1950s a young woman like me couldn't imagine leaving on her own.

When we returned from summer in Europe a letter from Sam was waiting. Would I visit him over Christmas break? He met me at the Greyhound terminal and drove me to the family home. His mother was sweet, older sister friendly, and father acceptably welcoming behind his constant highball breath. The closest Sam got, over the years, to sharing his childhood trauma was mention of a feared hair brush—perhaps his father's weapon of choice. Sometimes he dreamt about that brush. The next morning the rash would be worse. He favored brown cotton work shirts, an indelible unguent discoloring all their sleeves.

On that visit I lost my virginity, and did indeed feel something had been lost. Or perhaps just nothing gained. Sam asked if the sex hurt, a question meant to be reassuring. I told him no. And I didn't complain when he sent me home a day early, confidently explaining he had a date with a "hot" girl he just had to see. I boarded my bus with his hockey stick in hand. The thick black tape wound about its long handle conjured a mysterious sense of belonging.

The letters continued and, two months later—February, 1954—, we eloped to Ciudad Juárez, six hours south of Albuquerque just over the Mexican border. Not a total elopement, since we'd told my parents where we were headed. His didn't know. I wore a periwinkle blue knit skirt and sweater, the latter with a fuzzy angora mock turtleneck collar, my favorite outfit at the time. In Las Cruces we stopped to buy rings. Sam chose a plain band in white gold, I a narrower yellow one. Together they set us back $19. After a few days his father appeared. He tried to persuade Sam to have the marriage annulled. The son stood up to the father, and I remained Mrs. Sam Jacobs.

The end of my first semester of college saw me looking for a job. Clearly it was more important for the man to study than the woman. Besides, I already knew I was going to be a writer. Sam started philosophy, switched to geology and then music. He'd exude enthusiasm until something new caught his fancy. The one constant was his belief that he knew everything and was always right. I learned to justify his bravado and cover for his mistakes. He worked too. I especially remember a milk route because there wasn't a single week his accounts weren't off, sometimes a few dollars over, more often several short.

We lived in an efficiency apartment on Copper, a single room on the second floor of a square white building in the middle of an empty lot. I baked casseroles of Campbell's Cream of Celery Soup and canned tuna topped with grated cheese. Smelling of beer and rotten teeth, the aging landlord would come by each month for the rent. Once I opened our door in my long yellow bathrobe and when I held out the money he wouldn't let go of my hand. Voicing my fear would have been unthinkable.

Sam was bored with life in Albuquerque, so I was bored. He decided we would travel to India. Despite our not having had a big wedding, friends of both families had legitimized our union with the usual gifts: the pressure-cooker, vacuum cleaner, pots and serving platters of every material and shape. We sold them all and got enough to buy a Lambretta motor scooter, sister to the Vespa but, Sam assured me, a much better deal for the price. I didn't question his judgment. We had $400 left over, a small fortune in the mid 1950s.

We rode off one morning, outfitted with backpacks and sleeping bags from our local Army Surplus store, my family waving goodbye until we disappeared out old Route 66 to the east. I remember little of the trip across country, or even of our transatlantic crossing on one of the Holland America ships. Memory remains sharper of our trip down through central Europe, from Rotterdam to Belgium and across the Pyrenees into Spain. We'd named our scooter Friendly. She did 35 miles per hour, tops.

We never made it to India. By the time we reached southern Spain our money was almost gone. Hitting an oil slick on narrow pavement damaged Friendly enough that we had to take her across to Genoa, Italy for repairs. I remember sitting for a week in a dim garage, trying hard to coax elemental Italian from poorly-learned high school Spanish. Genoa was filled with buildings of black and white striped marble. Youth hostels and student eateries were as plentiful there as they'd been through central Europe.

Soon, though, we were broke. Our scooter fixed, we ended up in Madrid. The extremes of Sam's belligerence surfaced when he tried to talk me into prostituting myself for food. I preferred scavenging through garbage cans while he adjusted to my first refusal to do what he thought best. After a month I found work: as a maid at a student boarding house. I have never forgotten its address: Calle Magallanes #19. Occupying half an apartment building floor, it was a large place with rooms up and down one long hall. I cleaned and made beds; Sam ran errands. We slept in the kitchen on a narrow fold-down metal cot.

Soon the woman who owned the pensión asked if I could also do the food shopping. By this time I had made friends with some of the prostitutes who lived in our floor's other apartment. They mostly worked at night and slept during the day, and one of them—Juana—was happy to take me with her to the market, pointing to each item and slowly pronouncing its name until my utilitarian Spanish improved. Juana and I became friends. After a particularly brutal police raid, I visited her in jail. I cried when I saw her shaved head.

Sam eventually found a job in the southern city of Seville. The U.S. was building a military base and hiring civilians to work on an oil pipeline there. We must have found out about the possibility at the Embassy in Madrid; back then young travelers like us frequented our country's embassies in search of aid or information. We ended up living in Seville for more than a year, in a rooftop apartment in the tree-lined Barrio Santa Cruz which we shared with a Swede named Bo and John from New Jersey.

I grew a lot that year. The living situation broadened my knowledge of places and people, and allowed me to imagine life without Sam. One day, while my husband was at work, Bo and I crawled into bed together. I was looking for sex without violence. We just lay there, beside one another and fully clothed. Still, for me the unconsummated event bore the shame of early transgression.

But even with Sam the time in Seville offered a lot. We met a group of Flamenco dancers at a club called El Patio Andalúz, and traded the young men and women English lessons for classes in dance. Sam dabbled in Flamenco guitar. Before we left Seville the club's owner put us in the backup cuadro for a week.

We returned to Albuquerque, and with the money we'd saved in Spain bought a tiny house, a compact square containing living room, bedroom, kitchen and bath. It was on Grove Street NE, out by the Fair Grounds, and a high pumice block wall surrounded the back yard. Sam's boxer accidentally hanged herself trying to jump that wall: the rope he had left her on was too long or not long enough.

In later years I sold that house for $10,000. Since my more recent return to Albuquerque I tried to find the old place, until I realized several blocks of Grove no longer existed as a residential neighborhood; the state fair grounds had swallowed them whole.

I went back to work, this time for an engineering company that wrote operation and maintenance manuals for the Redstone and other missile programs. New Mexico was a hub of military activity. I even had top secret clearance. I remember we couldn't use typewriter ribbons more than once on that job, having to dispose of them through the narrow slots in locked trash cans. Sam went back to school.

My husband's instability began showing itself more frequently. He sought a therapist who happened to be experimenting with LSD, and suffered a psychotic break.

When Sam was okay, life together seemed possible. Sometimes he played music with my father and his friends. My parents pretended to like him. When he wasn't okay, I did my best to preserve the mask. I made an appointment with the surgeon who had operated on my mother's cancer; he was the only doctor I knew. When I told him I had come to talk about hating sex, he stopped looking directly at me and wrote the name of a book on a prescription blank, then shoved it across his desk. The book was *The Joy of Sex*. I bought a copy. Sam was enthusiastic but it didn't help.

Sam's parents visited us and we spent a few days at Red River Valley in the northern part of New Mexico. By this time they had accepted me as their daughter-in-law, despite our inauspicious beginnings, stark class difference, and my own parents' less than enthusiastic response to anyone Jewish. Sitting together at a picnic table in that mountain retreat Elizabeth waxed intimate. She asked what kind of a husband Sam was. Wonderful, I lied.

But he wasn't wonderful, and neither was our marriage. After several more emotional crises, I decided his family was better equipped than I to care for him. He was in a local sanitarium when I called them to say I'd had enough; would they please come and take him home? Released from the hospital, just before leaving town, he managed to burn every piece of writing I'd produced to date. I was left with all our material possessions.

I remember filing for divorce down at the old Albuquerque Court House. I wore red, and paid an extra $100 for the return of my maiden name. Twenty-one, and alone—or free—depending on how it felt from day to day.

And that might have been the end of Sam in my life. Except it wasn't.

After I'd moved to New York I got a call one day from Sam's cousin Jean. We'd met briefly during the marriage. Now she said Sam was doing well, still institutionalized but with weekend passes, and he'd like to visit if I was willing. We met at a West Village Theater where Brecht's "Three Penny Opera" was enjoying a long run. After the show we had drinks at a bar across the street. We talked for several hours. I remember the meeting as awkward and sad.

That was the last time I saw Sam. But some thirty years later a chance encounter wrote the final chapter to this story. I had given a poetry reading at the University of California, Santa Barbara. As the large auditorium began to empty I noticed a woman, sitting alone, who didn't appear to be leaving. I was about to exit when she approached, introducing herself as Elaine. "I'm Sam Jacobs' widow," she began.

Elaine wanted to fill me in on Sam's life after our marriage. She told me he had been married a second time before they met, but not for long. He had managed to make it through the rough years, gone back to school, and earned a doctorate. She had family photo albums. Sam had been an Assistant Professor of Ergonomics at UC Santa Barbara, where his colleagues and students loved him. Then, in 1977 at the age of 42, he died quite suddenly of a heart attack He left two young daughters, Dasha and Shira. "Ours was a happy marriage," Elaine told me. "He always felt badly about how he treated you."

In the dream a flock of blackbirds make off with my head. But nothing is really lost. Blue sky propels me to wakefulness.

Penitente Morada

Weapon and Signature

When I was young an occasional murder
upped the sales of our hometown paper
two or three days running.
Newspapers were important then
and violent death
an equal-opportunity visitor
claiming men and women,
poor and unprotected.

Sixty years later Internet sound bites
replace those papers,
TV conquers radio.
Scan the story, file the news
and move on.
Corporate control determines
how much we know
and for how long.

Murder, alive and healthy, makes its way
from the five-year-old
wielding his father's loaded gun
through post office or high school rampage
to the killing fields of war
and back.
The greater the human interest
the longer the public gasp.

Just south of these purple canyons
and clean skies
six hundred murdered women
on their way to school or work
haunt the streets of Juárez.

In every Mexican City, down to Guatemala
and north to Canada
dead women cry out
for someone to speak their names
without prostitute
or sweat shop worker
attached.

On Albuquerque's west mesa
the bones of eleven females
and one unborn child
rise through the leveled sands of development.
Every day they dig
costs corporate millions.
More of us accused in death
of living the dangerous life.

As long as they make sure we know
it's our oldest profession,
our fault,
like when they raped us
because our skirts were too short
or dress provocative.

Organized crime, drug cartel, power's sadism
changes its name
from country to country,
disappearing women
until they are found in garbage dumps
or shallow desert graves.

Our sisters continue to die,
their names silenced in a time
when the erasure of women
is weapon and signature:
harbinger of what's to come.

Elaine

In my early years here in New Mexico, the person who most radically redirected my life was a visitor. More than any native, she taught me where I was and where I could go. All I needed was courage. Simply knowing her provided an abundance of that. Elaine de Kooning took one look at our watermelon mountains, cottonwood trees and old adobe houses and made herself at home. She took one look at me and brought me under her wing.

Elaine was a brilliant artist and sensually expansive woman, unashamed of those desires I'd been taught to hide between folds of unease and deception. Dance had made her fulsome body graceful and lithe, her muscled arms always reaching toward the work in progress. In the 1950s young girls were taught never to admit what we longed for. Boys were supposed to make the first move, and trouble stuck like river slime to the girls who succumbed or let them "go all the way." Although my aunt and her life companion lived together in Santa Fe, the word lesbian remained unspoken.

My own mother nurtured a succession of extra-marital affairs in awkward frenzy, semisilence shrouding her frequent indiscretions. Elaine was the first woman I met who spoke openly and with disarming candor about desire; when several years after we met I headed for New York, she offered a long list of friends but warned me away from the occasional lover with whom she shared a special bond.

But intelligence and sex weren't the only or even most important arenas in which Elaine's outgoing nature redrew my interior map. Her identity in art, and attitude toward its process and practice, realigned my creative energies. As a visiting professor at our university's art department, her studio classes were always full. We met when I modeled for one of them, and she urged me to try my own hand at rendering the human figure.

Elaine believed in freedom. Freedom of gesture, risk in everything she touched. She showed me that abandon long practiced becomes skill. I remember great rolls of butcher paper. She would tear off a large swatch and tell me to keep my eye on what I was drawing, be bold in my stroke, aim for attitude rather than detailed representation.

There were lessons about materials as well: only the best brushes and most expensive paints would do. Especially for beginners, Elaine always said. Good materials were particularly important for those who couldn't yet harness talent. Unless you knew what that lush exuberance felt like in your hand, how could you know what making art could be? Elaine's generosity led to her providing the best for many young artists: an expertly stretched canvass or $50 brush. You were hooked by the time you understood that discipline was as necessary as pigment.

Like many from New York City, when she came to New Mexico Elaine couldn't drive. She bought a second-hand car and I and several others took turns teaching her to maneuver its idiosyncrasies. Drunk one night, she drove into her own living room. Passing her driving test was a problem. On her third try the traffic inspector was Irish. She beguilingly convinced him a third failure would discredit their shared national origin and obtained her license.

Later, in New York, throughout the years of our friendship I often dropped in on Elaine at her loft: sweatshop illegally turned living quarters and painting space combined. She continued painting while we talked, gossiped, laughed, conspired. Even as she stepped back from a work in progress, contemplating a problem area with the great power of intuition and analysis she honed throughout her life, her attention to our conversation was deeper and more to the point than what I got from anyone else. She went straight for the throat.

Elaine loved life. When I gave birth to Gregory she showered him with adoration and me with a year's worth of diaper service and anything else she could think of that would

Elaine de Kooning, 1980s

ease a single mother's life. Through Elaine my son became the mascot of the New York art world, attending gallery and museum openings in his white wicker basket. She thought his every move amazing.

Life for Elaine was just as valuable at the other end. When Caryl Chessman was condemned to die in California, Elaine threw herself into the campaign to save him. When he was executed she took to bed for a week. At every point along life's way, Elaine found reason to encourage and support all those who needed an injection of confidence, or save someone in danger of falling into the abyss. When my son was small and I needed the occasional babysitter, she explained how important hiring a recovering addict would be for the man's self-esteem. What more precious to entrust him with, she asked, than a beautiful baby? When a couple we knew couldn't take care of their little girl, Elaine found a childless couple in Texas to adopt her. If it favored human well-being, she could and would make anything happen.

Elaine never mentioned her father, except when she told the story of her mother leaving him. Marie was the traditional Irish Catholic and faithful mother of four until her children could make it on their own, but Elaine said she'd always been very clear she would take off one day. She'd even announced the future date, which no one took seriously. When that day came, she packed her bags and left. Once she no longer had to care for family, studying math and languages consumed the years she had left. Elaine said she was brilliant, and loved telling stories about the woman who had birthed her and was so ahead of her time. To her a woman going after what she needed and wanted was always to be celebrated.

Marie was proud of Elaine's accomplishments, although abstract expressionism was beyond her. I remember the day she found a larger than life-sized photo of Chessman's face among her daughter's things; it was mounted on canvass and had been used in a march against capital punishment. Marie said she was thrilled Elaine had returned to realistic portraiture.

This was long before the second wave of feminism swept many of us into its fervor. Like most of her female peers, Elaine didn't care to be called a woman artist. She was an artist, no more no less, and good as any man. The language of feminism wasn't something she ever adopted, yet whenever we talked about how women had to struggle for our rights, she was the first to admit the unfairness of society's gender assignments.

Elaine's sister Marjorie was her best friend and only true confidante, as well as the mother of the three nephews she showered with her own maternal exuberance. Her brothers Conrad and Peter were ready in the wings, part of that Irish family support that always seemed to bolster her. They too had children—I remember Peter's daughter Maude, a name that nestled in my consciousness—but Marjorie's Luke, Jon Pierre, and Mike were the clear inheritors of Elaine's largesse, and beneficiaries of her bountiful example.

In New Mexico my friendship with Elaine ushered me into a larger world, a dimension I've inhabited since. It was a world in which the most generous ideas were nurtured and what was off-limits for many seemed matter of fact. This included political concepts out of favor at the time. Art was valued, honesty was a virtue and anything was possible. If you came to Elaine with a problem, before you finished telling her about it she was actively involved in its solution. If you wondered whether to go this way or that, Elaine laughed and asked, "Why choose?"

In her early twenties, Elaine decided Willem de Kooning was the greatest painter of her generation. It was only logical they should fall in love and marry. She went with him to the experimental college at Black Mountain, North Carolina, and together they returned to New York City and a life of mid twentieth century cutting-edge creativity. There was no question in Elaine's mind that Bill was the best. Long after they no longer lived together—he involved with a succession of other women and she with her own lover of the moment—she devoted her considerable talents to promoting his career. Elaine thought and wrote about art as brilliantly as she made it.

In her forties, her stint in New Mexico established a connection that remained vital as long as she lived. Her presence, friendship and encouragement touched and changed many local artists, sending us on paths we might not have had the courage to explore had she not made us believe they were our natural next steps. The vast blue sky and desert palette, for her, were canvasses upon which the surprising and magical happened.

Here ancient cultures and contemporary indigenous communities welcomed her home. At the Zuni Shalako one year we spent the night with the pueblo's governor and his family. He was an admirer of Willem de Kooning's work. His mother—I think Lewis was her last name—had been the first woman from Zuni to earn a college degree. Elaine and I spent that night in sleeping bags under the broad portal of the governor's home, rising at dawn to watch the dancers coming across the plain from a distant mountain retreat. Later she got Bill to send the governor a small painting in gratitude.

I had already dispensed with a first sad marriage during which my young husband and I had lived for a while in Spain. That's where I fell in love with bullfighting, influenced by Hemingway's romantic novels and my own early attraction to pageantry. Back in New Mexico I drove regularly to Ciudad Juárez, the Mexican border city six hours south, to attend Sunday fights at its Plaza Monumental. For a while I even wrote fight reviews for a California magazine dedicated to the brutal rite.

Elaine and I spent many weekends together in Juárez. We always stayed at the same hotel, drank tequila at the same bar, and gloried in the Sunday afternoon display with its bravado and theater. Young and unperturbed by such cruelty to animals, I still subscribed to the excitement of the dubious drama with its predetermined outcome. Elaine would spend the entire afternoon sketching the dramatic movements of bejeweled fighter and angry animal. Those sketches led to one of her best-known series of paintings; and they in turn to her fascination with much more ancient bulls. Creative chutzpah gained her entrance to the caves at Lascaux long after they were closed to the public.

Elaine also loved painting athletes—loved the male body in action—and in New York we often went to Madison Square Garden to watch basketball or track. I remember going with her to see U.S. American John Thomas and Soviet Valery Brumel compete with one another. It was Brumel's birthday and he jumped seven feet six inches, extraordinary for the early 1960s. Later she did a portrait of President John F. Kennedy, spending many hours sketching him as he went about the affairs of state. When I lived in Cuba she asked if I thought I could wangle her a chance to paint Fidel. I tried but didn't succeed.

Years passed. I lived in Mexico, Cuba and Nicaragua before returning to New Mexico in 1984. Elaine continued to paint and show, earning a place for herself among the male artists—albeit inevitably a secondary place. One of Bill de Kooning's lovers gave birth to the child Elaine always dreamed of but never had. She and he continued to live separately, although joined by an unbreakable bond; toward the end of his life she moved back in, got him to stop drinking as she had years before, and jealously oversaw his care. By then dementia had taken much of Bill's mind, yet he continued to paint every day. She didn't need language to predict his needs. Then, surprisingly, she died before he did, consumed by the cigarettes she never could give up.

When the U.S. government tried to deport me because of ideas expressed in a number of my books, Elaine took a portrait of me she had done in 1960 and reproduced it as a high quality poster to be sold to benefit my struggle. She hadn't dated the image back when she painted it, and just before sending it to the printer added her signature "E de K" and "1963" at the bottom. I knew she'd painted it in 1960; I was pregnant with Gregory at the time. I told Elaine I was sure of the earlier date but she stubbornly stuck to 1963.

The last time Elaine and I saw one another she must already have been ill, but hid it well. I visited her at the beautiful East Hampton home and studio where she lived in later years. I'd brought some of my photographs and we made a trade. By this time I was living with a woman. I introduced my partner, and Elaine looked me straight in the eye and assured me she knew exactly why two women might choose to be together: there weren't that many good men anymore, she said. For the first and only time in our long friendship I made a conscious decision not to dispute the observation. There was too much else to talk about.

Downtown Albuquerque, art nouveau detail

Women I Would Never Be

Mute half century gone,
earned voice
calls crime by name today,
mourns its victims, vows
"we can never allow"
and on and on:
the slippery promises.

I lived this raging arc
from boys will be boys
to here I am, my life
crashed along its fault lines,
bent, broke beneath its weight,
struggled to stand again,
washed (almost) clean
by hot cascade of tears.

Language tells us who we are
but no one counts
beads faded on a rosary
mocking us stage left.

As long as we know
it was our fault,
small birds still crowd our mouths,
crack teeth, force us
to swallow before we chew.

Language shapes our world
and place within it.
It names us
but its words
may fall short, betray.

What of those gone to silence,
the women I would never be,
choices
withering in my garden even now?

Eva's Corn

Unburdened

Just north of the city, on Cochiti land,
fairy cones embrace a narrow canyon
where force of water and wind
shape undulating secrets.

As the sun rises in open sky
light bathes rock swirls
spilling pink and orange and purple
into its narrow crevices.

Like Antelope further north
a radiant dance
pulls answers to new questions
from the darkness of earth.

Growing up we were taught
which questions to ask
and which answers
brought success.

No one pointed us to slot canyons
slicing earth, drawing light
to reveal different questions
or answers unburdened by fear.

Tent Rocks, north of Albuqerque

Verdant

Verdant has her eye on me,
color and promise
at home in a tropical rainforest
Ireland's emeralds
or clinging to the moss-covered face
of a boulder bleeding morning dew.

As cross-wind of my desert
as dancing dolphins
or African lion,
verdant whispers look
and I fall into moist frenzy.

She sings to me and a ribbon of sound
begins in the pain
of my right foot's broken middle toe,
grows louder as it rises
through ankle, knee, thigh

exploding symphonic overkill
in my cracked lungs
then slowing to stillness as I close my eyes
remembering Precambrian seas
what my land was like millennia ago,
what place the seed of my seed
will inhabit next time around.

La Luz

The day I reached the top, a lifetime of sitting
burned the muscles of my calves.
I looked out beyond the city,
beyond the western mesa to extinct volcanoes
—line of dusky nipples tweaking horizon—
beyond Mount Taylor wrapped in Navajo prayer,
all the way to California.

Four thousand feet of switchback trail, eight miles
from desert to forested crest,
I needed a year and a half to advance by increments
through dry terrain of lower altitudes
past the turn where mountain stream
runs wet and dry and wet again
up to The Thumb

where two climbers we'd watched in their harnesses
died on the six o'clock news—how close
to our fascination, how briefly imprinted on our lives—
into the cooler upper mountain air,
back and forth across the rock slide
until the trail leveled off along knife's edge
through wooded highlands to the tram.

Sometimes we'd ride that tram up mountain
and hike down, others we'd start below
and make our slow way to the top.
Some days we'd round a bend in the trail
and startle a deer,
its deep brown eyes locked on ours,
its silence momentary trance.

Lizards and rabbits scurried from our step,
rattlers sunned themselves
on flat rocks or mid-trail.
Canyon wrens and peregrine falcons
offered their song
as we climbed farther, got higher,
accepted

the mountain's invitation to seasonal waterfalls,
a thousand bright blue butterflies
in one astonished cloud,
scrub cedar and piñon giving way
to oak and pine and ponderosa
as we lifted ourselves out of ordinary clutter
in twenty-first century America.

Despite a childhood of forged gym notes
and couch potato lethargy
I kept that date I didn't know I had.
Cacophony of mountain sound
reduced in my ears to a single note
until the birdcall or warning rattle
recognized themselves in me.

While it lasted, my mountain
taught me purpose and time,
answered any question.
Now that lungs fade
and muscle and sinew no longer do their work
I've learned to plant its memory
in the poem.

The Shorter Script

Return to a city releases those who died too young
to count off the markers of their lives,
Alice and Jack, Carlos "The Ragman"
who may have died before he left
or simply dreamed himself
a shorter script.

Herbie Goldman's daughter held forever
in Grand Canyon's rocky folds
released by a current colder than wind.
Bob and Bobbie's child lost from view,
sad Suzie Kurman
disappeared into madhouse maze.

Those I knew as a child, released in midlife or before
by a sudden split in the road, a place
that tasted different, closed their mouths
to desert sands.
They walk among us now,
warning us on.

Ever Ready to Fly

In years to come I'd learn the world could change,
follow a route of broken bodies
and searing hope,
seek those ridges of place and time
where travelers swallow fear
to carve impossible trails
through jungles of pain.

Growing up I knew nothing of red paint
aimed at the breasts of white doves
stenciled on Mexico's bullet-riddled walls,
nothing of kids not much older than me
dying for the crime of youth on Managua's streets,
throwing their only bodies
at generations of shame.

In 1953 I attended my city's whitest school,
dreamed of being homecoming queen,
wrote romantic poems
with church bells and tumbleweed
while Cubans I would embrace one day
made their first assault upon a dictator
who gave new meaning to an eye for an eye.

Words spoken only by desert rock back then,
words I neither heard nor understood,
wove a fabric keeping me warm in winter
and free of summer fevers
until I caught up with myself,
took risk in hand
and went in search of air.

Albuquerque accompanied me like a small tattoo,
bird or flower on my left shoulder,
this childhood city
where circumstance of birth
prepared me for nothing
but freed a spirit
ever ready to fly.

Dream Me

I want to believe statehood in 1912
dreamed my 1947 arrival

just as the city's seventeenth century plaza
dreamed today's cluster of skyscrapers,

or native inhabitants
living along the sinuous Río Grande

knew bearded men with guns and cross
would bring a time of terror and death.

What questions do we ask of our dreams?
What stories do they tell us
in the darkness of night?

The Thumb, Sandia Mountains

Margaret Randall is a feminist poet, writer, photographer and social activist. She is the author of over 80 books. Born in New York City in 1936, she has lived for extended periods in Albuquerque, New York, Seville, Mexico City, Havana, and Managua. Shorter stays in Peru and North Vietnam were also formative. In the 1960s she co-founded and co-edited *El Corno Emplumado / The Plumed Horn,* a bilingual literary journal which for eight years published some of the most dynamic and meaningful writing of an era. From 1984 through 1994 she taught at a number of U.S. universities.

Photo © 2010 by Janice Gould

Randall was privileged to live among New York's abstract expressionists in the 1950s and early '60s, participate in the Mexican student movement of 1968, share important years of the Cuban revolution (1969-1980), the first four years of Nicaragua's Sandinista project (1980-1984), and visit North Vietnam during the heroic last months of the U.S. American war in that country (1974). Her four children— Gregory, Sarah, Ximena and Ana— have given her ten grandchildren. She has lived with her life companion, the painter and teacher Barbara Byers, for the past two decades.

Upon her return to the United States from Nicaragua in 1984, Randall was ordered to be deported when the government invoked the 1952 McCarran-Walter Immigration and Nationality Act, judging opinions expressed in some of her books to be "against the good order and happiness of the United States." The Center for Constitutional Rights defended Randall, and many writers and others joined in an almost five-year battle for reinstatement of citizenship. She won her case in 1989.

In 1990 Randall was awarded the Lillian Hellman and Dashiell Hammett grant for writers victimized by political repression. In 2004 she was the first recipient of PEN New Mexico's Dorothy Doyle Lifetime Achievement Award for Writing and Human Rights Activism.

To Change the World: My Life in Cuba, was recently published by Rutgers University Press. "The Unapologetic Life of Margaret Randall" is an hour-long documentary by Minneapolis filmmakers Lu Lippold and Pam Colby. It is distributed by Cinema Guild in New York City.

Randall's most recent collection of poetry and photographs was *Their Backs to the Sea,* published by Wings Press in 2009.

For more information about the author, visit her website at www.margaretrandall.org.

Their Backs to the Sea

argaret Randall's *Their Backs to the Sea* is a major accomplishment from one of America's most radical poet-citizens. Randall travels here "beyond cobalt" and "beyond turquoise" to Rapa Nui to consider the implications of legend, lore, geography, geology, migration, conquest, slave economies, and the powerful, insistent and mysterious presence of the magnificent stone moai. whose backs are indeed to the sea. This stance—stoically away from—has far reaching implications for the investigative psyche, an inward twist toward a spiritual guardianship, perhaps. Who were they, those creators of the silent megaliths? Do empty sockets absent obsidian and coral "pull us into vacancy"? And who are we in our own craggy cliffs, in our own "disappearing pages of an ancient book"? Randall is here an "archeologist of morning" in the Olsonian sense, and invoked too is his stress on istorin, as the root of "history"—to find out for oneself. The book continues the braid of themes with further fierce inquiry from Baghdad to Chaco, north to Aztec and to powerful litanies of resistance. "Ridges are squeezed into giant fists" throughout. Randall's own photographs which thread the collection are powerful and stunning reclamations as well. Brava!"

> – Anne Waldman
> The Jack Kerouac School of Disembodied Poetics
> Naropa University

heir Backs to the Sea shows me again why I have looked to Margaret Randall for a poetry & a life driven by many forces, multiple times & places, changing with a will to change that places her among the real & really forceful poets of our time. Beginning with an extended poem in many parts – an epic as "a poem including history"—she first covers the archaeology & ecology of a chosen subject, Easter Island (Rapa Nui in the language of its people), then swings outward in these & other poems, to explore an even larger world & her own history as one who moves inside it. The book as book is breathtaking, both her words & her photographic studies that together jump genres, to leave us with a kinetic, truly complex work of art.

– Jerome Rothenberg
author of *Traditions of the Sacred*

Where do history and poetry meet to produce a third space of interrogation, wonder, and resonance? They do here. *Their Backs to The Sea* is a cartography of ruin, of contested days, of reclamation and occupation, of origin myths, of homage to the mysteries of an Easter Island both real and imagined, of lives lived in the center of time, of bodies who speak because language is life. In these poems, language travels through intricate tunnels where histories concenter to harmonize: do not forget the blood stained plaza of Tlatelolco, do not forget Komari the vulva glyphs, do not forget non-linear time, do not forget Auschwitz, do not forget absence of shame, do not forget life's other face. Mystery, resistance, and grace haunt these pages. It is a pleasure, yes, even in the face of atrocity and loss, a pleasure to travel these pages because the reader can be sure that the path is not without beauty. Margaret Randall is a rare poet—a seasoned historian who has not forgotten the primacy of the imagination.

– Akilah Oliver, author of *The She Said Dialogues: Flesh Memory*

The ease with which one moves through this clean, clear music masks the depth at which it works to change us as we read, enlarging an inner life to make room for so much experience—an exploration of the rim of Rapa Nui, an aging mother's death, the uprising in Mexico during the '68 Olympics. Margaret Randall writes poems of sympathy, intelligence, and witness. Listen to the small sounds, she tells us. Open your eyes. But the wonderfully negotiated distances between small sounds and clear sight generate the poetic sense here of a working world, a poet functioning in a functioning universe, the full specificity of what the poem can do today.

– Samuel R. Delany, author of *Dark Reflections*

Wings Press was founded in 1975 by Joanie Whitebird and Joseph F. Lomax, both deceased, as "an informal association of artists and cultural mythologists dedicated to the preservation of the literature of the nation of Texas." Publisher, editor and designer since 1995, Bryce Milligan is honored to carry on and expand that mission to include the finest in American writing—meaning all of the Americas, without commercial considerations clouding the choice to publish or not to publish. Technically a "for profit" press, Wings receives only occasional underwriting from individuals and institutions who wish to support our vision. For this we are very grateful.

Wings Press attempts to produce multicultural books, chapbooks, Ebooks, CDs, DVDs and broadsides that, we hope, enlighten the human spirit and enliven the mind. Everyone ever associated with Wings has been or is a writer, and we know well that writing is a trans- formational art form capable of changing the world, primarily by allowing us to glimpse something of each other's souls. Good writing is innovative, insightful, and interesting. But most of all it is honest.

Likewise, Wings Press is committed to treating the planet itself as a partner. Thus the press uses as much recycled material as possible, from the paper on which the books are printed to the boxes in which they are shipped.

As Robert Dana wrote in *Against the Grain*, "Small press publishing is personal publishing. In essence, it's a matter of personal vision, personal taste and courage, and personal friendships." Welcome to our world.

Colophon

This first edition of *My Town*, by Margaret Randall, has been printed on 60 pound EB Matte paper containing a high percentage of recycled fiber. Titles have been set in Colonna type, the text in Adobe Caslon type. All Wings Press books are designed and produced by Bryce Milligan.

On-line catalogue and ordering available at
www.wingspress.com

Wings Press titles are distributed to the trade by the Independent Publishers Group www.ipgbook.com and in Europe by www.gazellebookservices.co.uk